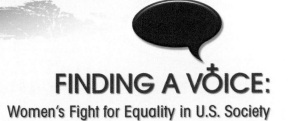

**FINDING A VOICE:**
Women's Fight for Equality in U.S. Society

# THE EQUAL RIGHTS AMENDMENT

LEEANNE GELLETLY

# FINDING A VOICE:
## Women's Fight for Equality in U.S. Society

# TITLES IN THIS SERIES

# THE EQUAL RIGHTS AMENDMENT

LEEANNE GELLETLY

MASON CREST
PHILADELPHIA

Dedicated to my great aunt Dora Gelletly Ogle,
who spent most of her life working for the legal rights of women.

**Mason Crest**
370 Reed Road, Suite 302
Broomall, PA 19008
www.MasonCrest.com

Printed and bound in the United States of America.

CPSIA Compliance Information: Batch #FF2012-5. For further information, contact Mason Crest at 1-866-MCP-Book.

First printing
1 3 5 7 9 8 6 4 2

Library of Congress Cataloging-in-Publication Data

Gelletly, LeeAnne.
  The equal rights amendment / LeeAnne Gelletly.
    p. cm. — (Finding a voice: women's fight for equality in U.S. society)
  Includes bibliographical references and index.
  ISBN 978-1-4222-2351-2 (hc) — ISBN 978-1-4222-2361-1 (pb)
  1. Women's rights—United States—Juvenile literature.  2. Feminism—United
States—Juvenile literature.  3. Equal rights amendments—United States—Juvenile
literature.  I. Title.
  HQ1236.5.U6G43 2012
  305.420973—dc23
                                                    2011043479

Publisher's note: All quotations in this book are taken from original sources, and contain the spelling and grammatical inconsistencies of the original texts.

**Picture credits:** Jimmy Carter Library and Museum: 42; the Gerald R. Ford Presidential Library: 3, 36; Library of Congress: 8, 11, 13, 15, 16, 17, 18, 19, 20, 23, 24, 26, 31, 32, 33, 37, 38, 55; photo courtesy of Marine Corps Base Camp Pendleton Combat Camera: 41; OTTN Publishing: 43, 50; © 2011 Photos.com, a division of Getty Images: 44; Franklin D. Roosevelt Presidential Library: 28; Sewell-Belmont House and Museum: 12; Mark Herreid / Shutterstock.com: 47; Harry Hu / Shutterstock.com: 49; Lev Radin / Shutterstock.com: 52, 53; U.S. Equal Employment Opportunity Commission: 48.

# TABLE OF CONTENTS

# INTRODUCTION

*A. Page Harrington, director, Sewall-Belmont House & Museum*

As the Executive Director of the Sewall-Belmont House & Museum, which is the fifth and final headquarters of the historic National Woman's Party (NWP), I am surrounded each day by artifacts that give voice to the stories of Alice Paul, Lucy Burns, Doris Stevens, Alva Belmont, and the whole community of women who waged an intense campaign for the right to vote during the second decade of the 20th century. The original photographs, documents, protest banners, and magnificent floor-length capes worn by these courageous activists during marches and demonstrations help us bring their work to life for the many groups who tour the museum each week.

The perseverance of the suffragists bore fruit in 1920, with the ratification of the 19th Amendment. It was a huge milestone, though certainly not the end of the journey toward full equality for American women.

Throughout much (if not most) of American history, social conventions and the law constrained female participation in the political, economic, and intellectual life of the nation. Women's voices were routinely stifled, their contributions downplayed or dismissed, their potential ignored. Underpinning this state of affairs was a widely held assumption of male superiority in most spheres of human endeavor.

Always, however, there were women who gave the lie to gender-based stereotypes. Some helped set the national agenda. For example, in the years preceding the Revolutionary War, Mercy Otis Warren made a compelling case for American independence through her writings. Abigail Adams, every bit the intellectual equal of her husband, counseled John Adams to "remember the ladies and be more generous and favorable to them than your ancestors" when creating laws for the new country. Sojourner Truth helped lead the movement to abolish slavery in the 19th century. A hundred years later, Rosa Parks galvanized the civil rights movement, which finally secured for African Americans the promise of equality under the law.

The lives of these women are familiar today. So, too, are the stories of groundbreakers such as astronaut Sally Ride; Supreme Court justice Sandra Day O'Connor; and Nancy Pelosi, Speaker of the House of Representatives.

But famous figures are only part of the story. The path toward gender equality was also paved—and American society shaped—by countless women whose individual lives and deeds have never been chronicled in depth. These include the women who toiled alongside their fathers and brothers and husbands on the western frontier; the women who kept U.S. factories running during World War II; and the women who worked tirelessly to promote the goals of the modern feminist movement.

The FINDING A VOICE series tells the stories of famous and anonymous women alike. Together these volumes provide a wide-ranging overview of American women's long quest to achieve full equality with men—a quest that continues today.

The Sewall-Belmont House & Museum is located at 144 Constitution Avenue in Washington, D.C. You can find out more on the Web at www.sewallbelmont.org

This illustration, titled "The Sky Is Now Her Limit," was published less than two months after the Nineteenth Amendment, which gave women the right to vote, became federal law on August 26, 1920. Above the "Equal Suffrage" rung of the ladder are higher rungs with such labels as "Wage Equity" and "Positions of Trust." The Equal Rights Amendment to the U.S. Constitution was intended to facilitate women's progress toward these ideals.

# 1

# EQUAL RIGHTS

In 1923 a group of women came together in Senecca Falls, New York. They were celebrating a special anniversary. There were colorful pageants. And there were many speeches. Some paid tribute to two women—Lucretia Mott and Elizabeth Cady Stanton. In 1848 the two helped organize a convention on women's rights. It took place in Seneca Falls. And it became known as the Seneca Falls Convention. That event sparked the effort to win women the right to vote. Seventy-five years later Seneca Falls would also be the birthplace of the Equal Rights Amendment.

## THE NATIONAL WOMAN'S PARTY

One of the women at the 1923 conference was Alice Paul. As head of the National Woman's Party (NWP) in 1916, she had helped lead the campaign to gain the vote for women. The NWP worked to pass a voting rights amendment. It lobbied members of the U.S. Congress. It circulated petitions. And it organized tours of suffrage speakers.

But the NWP was best known for its militant tactics. Under Paul's leadership, NWP members picketed the White House. They demonstrated before congressional offices. Many of them were arrested. Some went to jail. Several prisoners, including Paul, went on hunger strikes. They wanted to pressure President Woodrow Wilson and members of Congress to support women's suffrage. (*Suffrage* refers to the right to vote.) The efforts of the NWP got a lot of attention.

# THE FIGHT FOR FULL EQUALITY

In 1919 Congress finally passed the Nineteenth Amendment. It guaranteed women the basic right of citizenship. It gave them the vote. The Nineteenth Amendment was ratified on August 20, 1920. (*Ratification* is the process in which an amendment becomes part of the U.S. Constitution. It requires approval by three-quarters of the states.) It was signed into law six days later.

But Alice Paul thought the Nineteenth Amendment was not enough. The following September, she told the *New York Times*:

> It is incredible to me that any woman should consider the fight for full equality won. It has just begun. There is hardly a field, economic or political, in which the natural and unaccustomed policy is not to ignore women. . . . Unless women are prepared to fight politically they must be content to be ignored politically.

# A NEW CAMPAIGN

In the early 1920s women did not receive the same guarantees under the law as men. State statutes and court decisions discriminated against them. Men received preferential treatment. This was especially true in cases involving divorce, child custody rights, and property rights. In some states, laws barred women from serving on juries.

The National Woman's Party turned to helping women achieve more rights. Its focus was on feminism. *Feminism* refers to the advocacy of social, political, and economic equality of women and men. And one way to publicly support women was to abolish laws that discriminated against them.

At first the NWP had its lawyers identify problem state laws. Then they worked on drafting replacement bills. These new laws ensured that women and men were treated equally. The model bills were given to state legislatures. And the NWP lobbied to have the measures introduced. Some bills called for admitting women to jury service. Others guaranteed equal guardianship rights of children. Still others promoted equal treatment in cases of divorce.

# THE EQUAL RIGHTS AMENDMENT

But Paul soon decided that a Constitutional amendment was needed to guarantee a woman's equal rights under the law. At the 1923 Seneca Falls meeting, she called on Congress to pass a new amendment. She read aloud the one she had helped write. It stated, "Men and women shall have equal rights throughout the United States and in every place subject to its jurisdiction."

## ALICE STOKES PAUL (1885–1977)

Raised in a Quaker home, Alice Stokes Paul grew up believing in equality of men and women. She graduated from Swarthmore College in 1905. And she went on to study in England. There, she learned militant tactics of the British suffrage movement. They included the use of pickets, parades, and demonstrations. After returning to the United States, Paul became a leader in the suffrage movement. And she used tactics learned in England to fight for the vote in America.

After ratification of the Nineteenth Amendment, Paul dedicated her life to obtaining equal rights for women. She was one of the original authors of the Equal Rights Amendment. And she often served as spokesperson for the NWP's work on the ERA. She frequently testified before Congress in its support.

During the 1920s and 1930s Paul worked for women's rights internationally as well as nationally. In 1938 she founded the World Woman's Party, which had its headquarters in Geneva, Switzerland. The group promoted equal rights for women around the world.

After the National Woman's Party launched its campaign to pass an Equal Rights Amendment, it renamed its weekly journal. It had been called *The Suffragist*. In 1923 the publication was renamed *Equal Rights*. The journal was published from February 1923 until November 1954.

Paul told the audience why an amendment was needed. She insisted, "We shall not be safe until the principle of equal rights is written into the framework of our government." The attendees agreed. They decided to work for passage of the amendment. They did so "in order to bring the complete equal rights ideal to the victory that was won for suffrage."

That December Daniel R. Anthony, Jr., introduced the amendment in the U.S. House of Representatives. He was the nephew of famed suffrage leader Susan B. Anthony. The Senate Republican whip, Charles Curtis, introduced the amendment in the Senate. It would be known as the Equal Rights Amendment.

The Equal Rights Amendment would be introduced in every session of Congress that followed. But it remained in committee in both houses. After a bill or amendment is introduced, it must

Dora Gelletly Ogle (1882–1960) was a founding member of the National Woman's Party and served as the business manager of the organization's weekly journal *Equal Rights*.

U.S. Rep. Daniel R. Anthony (1870–1931) and Senator Charles Curtis (1860–1936) introduced the Equal Rights Amendment in Congress during 1923. However, opponents of the legislation kept the bill tied up in committee, preventing Congress from voting on the ERA.

be reviewed by a committee. After hearings are held, committee members vote on whether to send it to the floor of the House or Senate. There, debate continues. And the measure is ultimately voted on.

However, a committee chair can refuse to place a bill or resolution on the agenda. Or the chair can refuse to report a bill. If the bill is buried in committee, the full House will not be able to consider it.

The wording of the ERA would change in 1943. But its intent remained the same. The amendment would guarantee women equality under the law.

# FAST FACT

Alice Paul called the measure she helped write the Lucretia Mott Amendment. She was honoring one of the first women to call for equality for women. Lucretia Mott (1793–1880) devoted her life to working for women's rights.

# 2

# PROTECTIVE LABOR LAWS

Some people did not want an Equal Rights Amendment. Among them were some women who had worked to win the vote. They did not think the amendment was needed. And they worried that it would overturn laws intended to help working women.

## PROTECTIVE LEGISLATION

According to the U.S. Bureau of Labor, during the 1920s and 1930s there were 11 million women in the workforce. Two-thirds of them were working to help support their families. Some were married. Others were single, widowed, or separated from their husbands. Many were from low-income families.

Women made up the majority workforce in the garment and textile industries. These were factory jobs. They paid low salaries. They required long, hard hours. And they often took place in unsafe conditions. Children as young as six years old worked in factories, too.

Over the years, reform groups had fought to pass labor laws to help women and children. By the 1920s child labor was restricted. And many workplace safety laws were in place. Legislation limited the number of hours that a woman or child could work certain jobs. Other laws restricted the amount of weight women could lift. Some laws mandated rest periods.

Or they forbade women from working at night. The laws were meant to help women and children. So they were known as "protective legislation."

# ERA OPPOSITION

One group that had worked to pass protective legislation was the National Women's Trade Union League of America (NWTUL). This labor group had been founded in 1903 to improve working conditions for women. During the 1910s it had supported suffrage for women. But the NWTUL strongly opposed the ERA. Its leaders wanted to keep protective legislation. And the ERA would nullify any laws that applied only to women.

Young women at work in a Georgia mill spinning cotton thread, circa 1909. In the early 20th century, most jobs held by women were low-paying. Often, they involved long hours in dirty or dangerous factories. States passed protective legislation to limit the number of hours that a woman (or child) could work in certain jobs. Some states even guaranteed a minimum wage. The legal result, however, was that men and women were treated differently in the workplace.

# FAST FACT

The first protective legislation was passed in 1874 in Massachusetts. It restricted work hours for women and children mill workers to 10 hours per day. By 1900, 14 states had similar laws.

Another group opposed to the amendment was the League of Women Voters. This group included many former suffragists. The League had evolved from the National American Woman's Suffrage Association (NAWSA). Founded in 1890, NAWSA helped lead the fight to gain the vote. After the Nineteenth Amendment passed, its president, Carrie Chapman Catt, founded the League of Women Voters.

The seal of the National Women's Trade Union League features a woman in armor with a shield marked "Victory" taking the hand of a mother holding a child. Between them the sun rises over the organization's goals: "The Eight-Hour Day. A Living Wage. To Guard the Home." The NWTUL worked to pass minimum wage and maximum hours laws for women workers. And the group worked for laws to eliminate child labor. The NWTUL also helped workers establish the right to organize and engage in collective bargaining. The league organized labor strikes to call attention to workplace problems, especially in the garment industry.

Activist and union leader Ethel M. Smith is pictured in the front row, fifth from left, in this photograph of investigators with the Women's Bureau of the U.S. Department of Labor in Washington, D.C. As the NWTUL legislative secretary, Smith was a leader of the opposition to the ERA during the 1920s and 1930s.

The League worked to educate women to become active in government. And it provided information on campaign issues. And like the NWTUL, the League considered the ERA as a threat to laws protecting women and children. The group refused to support the new amendment. Instead, it called for specific legislation to end legal discrimination against women. Several decades would pass before the League would reverse its stand.

Another labor group opposed to the ERA was the Women's Bureau. This federal agency was founded in 1920. It was part of the U.S.

In 1932 Hattie Wyatt Caraway (1878–1950) became the first woman elected to the U.S. Senate. In 1933 she became the first woman to chair a Senate subcommittee. During her second term she cosponsored the Equal Rights Amendment.

Department of Labor. And it had been established to address the needs of working women. The Women's Bureau gathered employment data on women in the work force. And it provided information on labor legislation affecting women.

The Bureau worked closely with other women's organizations. They included the NWTUL, the National Consumers League, and the League of Women Voters. This coalition supported protective labor legislation for women. And it worked to stop passage of the ERA.

## SEX-BASED LEGISLATION

ERA supporters claimed that protective labor laws were not helpful for women. Such laws meant that women and men received different treatment. And that could limit a woman's opportunities. For example, a law might require a woman to work no more than an eight-hour shift. Employers who needed people to work overtime would prefer to hire a man because his work hours would not have legal restrictions. Protective legislation could cost the woman the chance to be hired.

The National Woman's Party opposed any sex-based legislation. Its position was that labor laws should apply to both men and woman. Or they should not exist at all. In 1926 the organization issued the statement:

> [P]rotective legislation that is desirable should be enacted for all workers. . . . Legislation that includes women but exempts men . . . limits the woman worker's scope of activity . . . by barring her from economic opportunity.

# FAIR LABOR STANDARDS

The 1930s saw great economic and social upheaval in the United States. The country was undergoing a severe economic downturn. It became known as the Great Depression. During the presidency of Franklin D. Roosevelt (1933–1945), new laws were passed to regulate labor issues. These were part of his reforms to help the U.S. economy. They were known as New Deal reforms.

One of these laws was the Fair Labor Standards Act of 1938. It set the minimum hourly wage at 25 cents. And the maximum workweek was limited to 44 hours. The Act also banned children under age 18 from working in jobs that were deemed dangerous. The new law was significant because it applied to

Frances Perkins arrives at the White House for a meeting with President Franklin D. Roosevelt, 1939. Perkins (1880–1965) was the first woman to serve in a president's cabinet. She was secretary of labor from 1933 to 1945.

During the late 1930s and early 1940s, a New York attorney and former suffragist named Dorothy Strauss (1888–1960) testified before Congress several times, advising legislators not to pass the Equal Rights Amendment. Strauss feared that passage of the ERA would lead to the removal of minimum wage and work-hour protections for working women. Strauss was a leader of the League of Women Voters in New York; that organization also opposed the ERA.

both men and women. But in its final form, the Act covered only businesses involved in interstate commerce. This meant it affected only about one-fifth of the labor force. The New Deal laws did not apply to agricultural jobs or to domestic workers. Women were majority workforce in these positions. As a result, many women did not benefit from the legislation.

## THE ALICE PAUL AMENDMENT

From 1923 to 1940 the Equal Rights Amendment was introduced into each session of Congress. But it was held in committee. In both the House and Senate it never reached the floor for a debate.

The NWP worked to get a major political party to support the amendment. Activists lobbied the Republicans and the Democrats. Every four years NWP delegations went to the presidential nominating conventions. They asked each party to support the ERA. But for many years neither political party would agree. Finally, in 1940, the amendment gained the support of the Republican Party. It agreed to include the ERA in its platform.

Meanwhile, Alice Paul consulted with lawyers. With their help the ERA was rewritten in 1941 to read:

> Equality of rights under the law shall not be denied or abridged by the United States or by any State on account of sex.

The proposed amendment was now known as the Alice Paul Amendment. In 1943 the Senate Judiciary Committee approved the measure. But it failed to receive enough votes in the House Judiciary Committee to be sent to the floor of the House of Representatives.

But the ERA continued to gain support. The following year the Democratic Party included it in its platform. And various professional groups for businesswomen, lawyers, and teachers also endorsed it. These groups included the National Federation of Business and Professional Women's Clubs (BPW), the National Association of Women Lawyers, and the National Education Association.

## GROWING SUPPORT FOR THE ERA

A turning point in the history of the Equal Rights Amendment came in 1940, when for the first time it was included in a major party's campaign platform. Yet its inclusion was an accident—women in the Republican Party had originally drafted a plank offering vague support for women's rights but not for the ERA. Unbeknownst to the female party leaders, a delegate from Oklahoma named Perle Mesta provided new language that endorsed the Equal Rights Amendment. "So it was substituted and read to the convention," recalled Alice Paul in the 1970s. "And all these [Republican] women said 'Well, who played this trick on us?' . . . And I said, 'Well, anyway it's in, and we certainly have to continue with it.' And very reluctantly they didn't stage any opposition."

The Republican Party's 1940 platform stated, "We favor submission by Congress to the States of an amendment to the Constitution providing for equal rights for men and women."

# EQUAL PAY

In 1941 the United States entered World War II. Soldiers headed off to war. And women took their places in steel mills and munitions factories. They became welders and riveters. They built airplanes and ships. But they earned less than men. Studies done during WWII revealed a problem of widespread wage discrimination.

In 1945 a group called the National Committee to Defeat the UnEqual Rights Amendment (NCDUERA) drafted a bill. It proposed that Congress pass a Women's Equal Pay Act. The NCDUERA had been organized by Women's Bureau personnel. Its members included labor groups, the League of Women Voters, and the Young Women's Christian Association. The NCDUERA goal was to do away with the need for an ERA. Passing a law to deal with the specific problem of wage discrimination would do this. This policy was referred to as "specific bills for specific ills."

The proposed law guaranteed women equal pay for equal work. Such laws existed already in two states. But no federal law had been passed. The federal Equal Pay Act would help women, and also leave existing labor protective laws intact.

The National Woman's Party opposed the bill. It maintained that laws should not pertain only to women. Any legislation should guarantee equal pay regardless of gender.

The Women's Equal Pay Act failed to pass in 1945. The war ended that year. Many legislators voted against the Act because of fears it would take jobs away from returning soldiers. Soon after, an estimated 2 million female workers in heavy industry lost their jobs to men returning from war. The traditionally "male" jobs went to men. And the policy of hiring men over women was reestablished. In some cases, new company regulations forbid the hiring of women who were married.

# SENATE ACTION

In July 1946 the ERA was debated on the Senate floor. It was the first time that the proposed amendment was considered since being introduced in

During World War II, the United States government encouraged women to enter the workforce. Women workers were needed to keep up production of critical war-related products so that American men could be sent overseas to fight. However, these workers were not paid the same wages as men.

Although Alice Paul described Arizona Senator Carl Hayden (1877–1972) as "very, *very* friendly to the cause of women," the change he proposed to the Equal Rights Amendment in 1950 made the legislation unacceptable to ERA supporters.

1923. After a three-day debate, the ERA came to a vote on July 19, 1946. But was defeated, 38 to 35. Because it was a Constitutional amendment, it had to receive two-thirds of the votes. This meant it needed 49 yes votes. It failed to pass by 11 votes.

In January 1950 the ERA was again debated on the floor of the Senate. This time a Democratic senator from Arizona, Carl Hayden, proposed an amendment to the amendment. His "rider" stated that the ERA would not weaken any existing protective legislation rights or benefits.

The Hayden rider was approved. And the ERA was then voted on. It passed the Senate by a vote of 63 to 19. But ERA supporters were disturbed. The added language effectively canceled the purpose of the original amendment—equal protection. So they were not disappointed when the House of Representatives did not take up the rider or the amendment.

## STUCK IN COMMITTEE

In the House of Representatives, the ERA never left the Judiciary Committee. A labor union supporter and Democrat from New York named Emanuel Celler chaired the committee. He strongly opposed the ERA. And he ensured that no hearings were held on it.

Labor unions continued their steady opposition to the ERA. And NWP lobbyists continued to work to have the amendment introduced into each session of Congress. The lobbyists educated legislators about sex discrimination. And they gained supporters. But the amendment remained tied up in committee. More than two decades would pass before the ERA was again debated in Congress.

# 3

# A CALL FOR CHANGE

The roles of women and men remained divided during the 1960s. Newspapers posted jobs by gender. Ads read "Help Wanted Male" and "Help Wanted Female." Men were hired as pilots, construction workers, and bus drivers. There were "women's jobs," too. They included positions as airline stewardesses, secretaries, and nurses.

## BARRIERS

Women would apply for "men's jobs." But because they were women, they were not hired. They could not become firefighters, police officers, plumbers, or electricians. Banking and law firms refused to employ them. Many professions and their associations prevented women from joining their ranks.

There were also legal barriers. Many laws did not treat women and men equally. Legal paperwork often required a husband's signature. Some laws specifically discriminated against women. For example, one Arizona law required that the governor, secretary of state, and treasurer had to be male. In Georgia, a wife was not her husband's legal equal. The state law read, "The husband is head of the family and the wife is subject to him."

# THE FEMINIST MOVEMENT

But job and legal discrimination was only part of the story. There were also cultural barriers in the 1960s. Young women were not supposed to get "too educated." That would make it hard for them to find a husband. Many people believed that a woman should hold only two roles—that of wife and mother.

One of the first to challenge this attitude was Betty Friedan. She was married. And she had three children. She was also college educated. And she worked as a journalist for several years. Friedan felt something was

## BETTY FRIEDAN (1921–2006)

Betty Friedan was a leading figure in the women's rights movement in the 1960s. She was born Betty Naomi Goldstein on February 4, 1921, in Peoria, Illinois. In 1942 she graduated from Smith College. She then studied psychology at the University of California at Berkeley. In 1947 she married Carl Friedan.

Friedan's book *The Feminine Mystique* was published in 1963. It began a conversation about women's place in U.S. society. Friedan went on to cofound the National Organization for Women. During the 1970s she worked for the ratification of the ERA.

In 1971 Friedan helped establish the National Women's Political Caucus. This group worked to increase women's participation in politics. Friedan also helped found the National Abortion Rights Action League. The organization worked for the repeal of abortion laws and supported a woman's right to end a pregnancy.

Friedan remained an activist her whole life. She wrote several more books on politics and women's issues. She died on February 4, 2006.

missing in the lives of suburban housewives. She called it "the problem that has no name."

Friedan studied women in U.S. society. She interviewed housewives. And she analyzed advertising. Ads in the early 1960s typically portrayed women as happy homemakers. But Friedan came to the conclusion that many homemakers were not happy. Millions of wives and mothers felt unfulfilled. They felt restricted by society's traditional roles for them. And they wanted more from life.

In 1963 Friedan published her observations. She called her book *The Feminine Mystique*. The book was an immediate best seller. It sparked a national debate about women's role in the family. And it helped inspire the feminist movement of the 1960s.

## STATUS OF WOMEN

At the same time the U.S. government was taking a closer look at women in the workplace. In 1961 John F. Kennedy was president. He had appointed a woman in his administration named Esther Peterson. She served as assistant secretary of labor. And she was director of the Women's Bureau.

Peterson was a former lobbyist for the labor union the American Federation of Labor-Congress of Industrial Organizations (AFL-CIO). Labor still did not support the Equal Rights Amendment. And neither did Peterson. She wanted to find another way to help women. So she recommended the creation of a special commission.

# FAST FACT

In early 1963 Congress passed the Equal Pay Act. The new law prohibited employers from giving men and women different salaries for the same jobs. The bill was signed into law by President Kennedy in June 1963. But it covered only about 60 percent of the female labor force.

Esther Peterson (right) served on the Presidential Commission on the Status of Women with Eleanor Roosevelt (1884–1962), an internationally recognized advocate for human rights. Peterson (1906–1997) had a long and distinguished career as a supporter of women's rights in the workplace.

The commission would review the status of U.S. women. It would identify barriers in the workplace. And it would make recommendations for handling them. Peterson believed the commission would solve women's employment issues. And it would eliminate the need for the ERA. Establishing the commission could end "the present troublesome and futile agitation over the ERA," she noted.

In December 1961 an executive order created the President's Commission on the Status of Women (PCSW). Peterson was a member. And former first lady Eleanor Roosevelt served as chair. Most PCSW members opposed the ERA. An exception was Marguerite Rawalt. She was president of the National Association of Women Lawyers. Rawalt was also a former president of the National Federation of Business and Professional Women's Clubs (BPW). The BPW had been an early supporter of the ERA.

# AMERICAN WOMEN

In October 1963 the PCSW issued its recommendations. The report, called *American Women,* documented discrimination against women. It reported that they received unequal pay. And it noted women lacked legal equality. The report pointed out the need for support services for working women. It called for changes in education, social security, childcare, and employment.

*American Women* did not endorse the ERA. In fact, it said that no such amendment was needed. The PCSW stated that women were already granted equality by the Fifth and Fourteenth Amendments. Both amendments have "equal protection" clauses. For example, the Fourteenth Amendment includes the phrase "nor shall any State . . . deny to any person . . . the equal protection of the laws."

Critics of the report disagreed that the Fourteenth Amendment provided equality for women. It was ratified in 1868. At the time, suffragists said it gave women the right to vote. But the courts did not agree. The amendment refers to the protection of "citizens" and "persons." But it also states that "persons" are defined as "male."

# CIVIL RIGHTS ACT OF 1964

The ERA still saw no action in Congress. But legal protection for women soon came with a new law. For many decades black Americans had suffered from racial discrimination. During the 1950s and 1960s they organized and held demonstrations to protest. African Americans called for laws to protect their civil rights. In November 1963 President Kennedy was assassinated, and vice-president Lyndon B. Johnson assumed the presidency. One of his

# FAST FACT

The PCSW report *American Women* was also published commercially. That edition included an introduction by anthropologist Margaret Mead.

first actions was to work for a strong civil rights act.

The original civil rights bill promised protection from discrimination on the basis of race, color, religion, and national origin. In February 1964 the bill was being debated in the House. That is when Congressman Howard W. Smith of Virginia proposed an addition. There were 11 sections, or titles, in the Act. Title VII prohibited discrimination in the workplace. Smith proposed that Title VII also protect "another minority group, the women." He asked that the word *sex* be added to "race, color, religion, and national origin."

When Smith made the suggestion, he did not seem serious. He made his amendment sound like a joke. Other House members copied his tone. Representative Martha Griffiths of Michigan was not amused. She noted, "I presume that if there had been any necessity to have pointed out that women were a second-class sex, the laughter would have proved it."

ERA backers supported the addition to Title VII. The National Woman's Party campaigned for its inclusion. Labor groups, including the Women's Bureau, opposed it. But on February 10, 1964, the Civil Rights Act as amended passed in the House.

The vote then went to the Senate. BPW members lobbied President Lyndon Johnson. And they sent telegrams to Senate Minority Leader Everett Dirksen. He did not want to include the reference to sex discrimination. He believed it would kill the bill. Dirksen wanted to see the Civil Rights Act pass. And it was already controversial.

A 75-day filibuster would hold up the vote. And the debate would be one of the longest in Senate history. But Dirksen left the amendment intact. And on June 10, 1964, the Civil Rights Act passed the Senate. President Johnson signed it into law the following month.

# EQUAL EMPLOYMENT OPPORTUNITY COMMISSION

The Act created a new federal agency. It was called the Equal Employment Opportunity Commission (EEOC). Its purpose was to hear complaints

During the 1960s Congresswoman Martha Wright Griffiths (1912–2003) of Michigan became a leading advocate of women's rights in the U.S. House of Representatives. She helped to make sure that the Title VII provision preventing discrimination on the basis of gender was included in the 1964 Civil Rights Act.

about discrimination. And it was to enforce the new law.

In its first year the EEOC received many complaints of discrimination. Not all were on the basis of race. About one-third of them involved sex discrimination in the workplace. But the EEOC did not deal with these cases. It tended to ignore the issue of gender discrimination.

# NATIONAL ORGANIZATION FOR WOMEN

In 1966 women activists decided to pressure the EEOC to enforce the law. That year they founded a new organization. It was called the National Organization for Women (NOW). Founder Betty Friedan served as its first president. Other NOW cofounders included Muriel Fox, Pauli Murray, Aileen Hernandez, and Richard Graham.

NOW called for women to have legal and economic equality with men. The group worked to pass legislation. It provided lawyers so women could take sex discrimination cases to court. It advocated support services like daycare and maternity leave. And it called for equal educational opportunities for women.

U.S. Rep. Emanuel Celler (1888–1981) of New York was a longtime opponent of the Equal Rights Amendment. He kept the bill tied up in the House Judiciary Committee from 1949 until 1971. His opposition to the ERA led to his defeat in the 1972 Democratic Party primary by a feminist candidate, Elizabeth Holtzman.

A controversial issue was a woman's reproductive rights. NOW advocated that a woman had the right to decide whether to end her pregnancy. So the group worked to repeal abortion laws. (*Abortion* refers to the medical procedure to end a pregnancy.)

But NOW's primary goal was passage of the ERA. Its members endorsed the amendment in 1967. And the group's lobbyists focused on Congress.

# DEBATE IN THE HOUSE

The head of the House Judiciary Committee, Emanuel Celler, had kept the ERA buried in committee. Hearings had not been held since 1948. But in June 1970 Representative Martha Griffiths forced a discussion. That is when she began collecting signatures for a discharge petition.

A discharge petition takes a proposed measure out of committee. That is, the committee's approval is no longer needed to send a measure to the floor of the House or Senate. But the petition requires signatures from half the membership, plus one more, of the respective legislative chamber. So it is unusual for one to succeed. But this one did. Hearings on the ERA began on August 10.

When Griffiths discussed the need for the ERA, she made sure to address labor's concerns. "Give us a chance to show you that those so-called protective laws to aid women—however well intentioned originally—have become in fact restraints," she said. Such laws " keep wife, abandoned wife, and widow alike from supporting her family."

Celler predicted the worst. "The adoption of a blunderbuss amendment," he said, "would erase existing protective female legislation with the most disastrous consequences."

But some labor groups had changed their stance. They now endorsed the measure. In the summer of 1971 members of the National Education Association voted at their convention to support the ERA. The United Auto Workers followed suit.

The following October the House approved the ERA. The vote was 354 to 24. In March 1972 the Senate took up the debate.

## DEBATE IN THE SENATE

The chair of the Senate Judiciary Committee, Sam Ervin, strongly opposed the ERA. He had spoken against the amendment the previous year. And as the Senate debated the ERA, he introduced changes. Each Ervin amendment was intended to protect the "traditional rights" of women. One kept female labor protection laws in place. Another preserved family and spousal rights. But each change was defeated.

On March 22, 1972, the Senate approved the ERA. The vote was 84 in favor, with 8 opposed. The amendment

Sam Ervin (1896–1985), a powerful U.S. senator from North Carolina, was strongly opposed to the Equal Rights Amendment. Although his 1972 attempts to change the amendment failed, he later lobbied the North Carolina legislature not to ratify the ERA.

# FAST FACT

In 1971 the U.S. Supreme Court ruled that the Fourteenth Amendment protected women from discriminatory treatment by state or military officials.

had three sections. The first section maintained the text from 1943. The second section gave Congress the power to enforce the amendment. And the third established the date it would take effect. A preamble to the amendment placed a seven-year time limit on the ratification process.

The full text of the ERA stated:

Sec. 1. Equality of rights under the law shall not be denied or abridged by the United States or any State on account of sex.

Sec. 2. The Congress shall have the power to enforce, by appropriate legislation, the provisions of this article.

Sec. 3. This amendment shall take effect two years after the date of ratification.

The ERA seemed to be on its way to becoming part of the U.S. Constitution.

# 4

# THE RATIFICATION CAMPAIGN

After passage of the Equal Rights Amendment in March 1972, it had to be ratified. This required approval by three-quarters of the states. There are 50 states. So ratification required the approval of 38 of them. Hawaii gave its okay within an hour. Three states followed the next day. Within a month 13 states had ratified the ERA. By the end of 1972, the number had reached 22. And by December 1973, 30 states had ratified.

## SUPPORT FOR RATIFICATION

Many women's groups promoted ratification. One was the League of Women Voters. (It had opposed the ERA in the 1920s. But it endorsed the amendment in 1954.) Another was the American Association of University Women. NOW and the National Woman's Political Caucus worked for the cause as well.

ERA supporters raised funds. They ran advertisements. And they held meetings to explain what the new amendment would do: It would end wage discrimination. It would prohibit the use of federal funds for boys-only or girl-only schools. It would protect the marital and property rights of women. And it would give women equal access to credit.

Newspapers published articles on the ERA. So did magazines. It was the subject of TV talk shows and other programs. Most stories were positive. Polls showed that the majority of Americans favored the ERA. And so did

U.S. President Gerald R. Ford proclaimed August 26, 1975, to be "Women's Equality Day." The date marked 55 years since the passage of the Nineteenth Amendment. Ford released a statement in which he encouraged Americans to ratify the Equal Rights Amendment. "In this Land of the Free, it is right, and by nature it ought to be," he said, "that all men and all women are equal before the law."

presidents. During the administrations of Gerald Ford (1974–1977) and Jimmy Carter (1977–1981), both men endorsed it.

But the ERA had its opponents. Many religious and conservative groups feared the changes the amendment would bring. They felt threatened by it. And they opposed ratification.

## THE OPPOSITION ORGANIZES

Phyllis Schlafly helped lead the anti-ERA effort. The conservative Republican published a political newsletter. It was called *The Phyllis Schlafly Report*. In February 1972 she published an essay opposing the ERA. It was entitled "What's Wrong with 'Equal Rights' for Women?" The following May she published "The Fraud Called the Equal Rights Amendment." Those essays were only the beginning. Schlafly's newsletter would feature more than a 100 anti-ERA articles.

Schlafly founded a "pro-family" organization. She called it the Eagle Forum. Later, she established another group. STOP ERA fought against ratification. People of many religious views supported STOP ERA. They included evangelical Christians, Mormons, Orthodox Jews, and Roman Catholics.

# ANTI-ERA MOVEMENT

Anti-ERA activists opposed the amendment for many reasons. They believed that making laws gender-neutral would hurt women. For example, some laws benefited women. They gave preference to the mother in child-custody cases. Or they granted alimony to women in cases of divorce. Such laws would be struck down.

Activists also said passage of the ERA would mean women could be drafted into military service. The draft had been around since the 1940s. By law, young men had to register for the military. Some were forced to enlist. The draft remained in effect until 1973. ERA opponents claimed that it could be reinstated. Ratification of the ERA would mean women could be drafted, too.

Members of Phyllis Schlafly's STOP ERA group protest against the amendment outside the White House, 1977. According to Schlafly, "STOP" stood for "Stop Taking our Privileges."

ERA foes also claimed the amendment would force the federal government to fund abortions. So supporting the ERA was viewed as promoting abortion. The issue gained more attention in January 1973. That is when the U.S. Supreme Court issued a decision in *Roe v. Wade*. The Court ruled that women had a constitutional right to have an abortion. The abortion issue helped fuel the growth of many anti-ERA groups.

Schlafly soon became a symbol of the anti-ERA movement. She spoke at meetings and rallies. She appeared on television talk shows. She said ERA

# PHYLLIS SCHLAFLY

Phyllis Stewart was born on August 15, 1924, in St. Louis, Missouri. In 1944 she received a bachelor's degree from Washington University. The following year she earned a master's degree in political science from Harvard. In 1949 she married lawyer Fred Schlafly. They had six children.

Schlafly first received national attention in the early 1960s. She self-published a book on politics. *A Choice Not an Echo: The Inside Story of How American Presidents Are Chosen* became a best seller. It was credited for helping Barry Goldwater win the Republican presidential nomination in 1964. Goldwater later lost the election to Lyndon Johnson. But the book cemented Schlafly's reputation as a conservative leader.

Schlafly ran for Congress unsuccessfully in 1952. (She would also run in 1970.) During the 1960s she held leadership roles with Republican women's groups in Illinois and nationally. In 1967 she began publishing *The Phyllis Schlafly Report*. As a political activist, she is often credited with the defeat of the ERA.

Although she stresses her role in life as a housewife, Schlafly has held many other roles. She is an author of several books on the family, feminism, and education. She also lectures and hosts a radio talk show.

# FAST FACT

The number of women in the workforce increased significantly from 1960 to 1980. It jumped from around 38 percent to more than 51 percent.

supporters were trying to destroy the family. She accused feminists of be-littling women who wanted to be wives and mothers. ERA supporters were "anti-family, anti-children, and pro-abortion," Schlafly said. "Feminists believe that the home was a prison and the wife and mother a prisoner."

## ERAMERICA

The anti-ERA efforts had an impact. In 1974 only three states ratified the ERA. Just one state ratified in 1975. And in 1976 no state legislatures rat-ified the amendment.

To help direct the ratification drive, ERA activists formed a new group. ERAmerica was founded in January 1976. Based in Washington, D.C., the coalition included representatives from 200 civic, labor, church, and women's groups. It was a political organization. But it included both Republicans and Democrats.

ERAmerica worked to sway support for the amendment in unratified states. It set up several campaigns. Target states included Illinois, Oklahoma, and several southern states. ERAmerica members lobbied state legislators. Volunteers organized rallies. And activists set up petition drives. ERAmerica did not have much funding. The bulk of the work was done through the efforts of volunteers.

## NATIONAL WOMEN'S CONFERENCE

In November 1977 a national women's conference took place in Houston, Texas. Two thousand women attended. Delegates came from every state. Speakers included feminist leaders like Gloria Steinem, Betty Friedan, and

NOW president Eleanor Smeal. U.S. congresswoman Bella Abzug served as chair. Also present were U.S. first ladies Rosalynn Carter, Betty Ford, and Ladybird Johnson.

Participants at the conference discussed issues affecting women. Calls were made to increase women's employment opportunities. Participants voiced support for the ERA. And the delegates passed several resolutions. One expressed support for gay rights. Another called for federal funding for abortion. Yet another supported government-sponsored childcare.

Conservatives opposed many of these resolutions. When the conference was held, STOP ERA held an opposition rally. It also took place in Houston. Schlafly criticized the "feminist convention." And she condemned the ERA campaign.

## ADDITIONAL OPPOSITION

The ERA had other foes. The insurance industry opposed the amendment for economic reasons. Insurance companies based their fees and payouts on gender. According to accident statistics, women had fewer accidents. So they were charged lower fees. But women received lower life insurance payouts than men did. This practice was based on the fact that women lived longer than men. If the ERA became law, companies would have to charge men and women the same fees and provide equal insurance payouts.

Other opponents to the ERA were states' rights supporters. The ERA gave Congress the power of enforcement. States' rights proponents

# FAST FACT

In the early 1970s labor groups concluded that protective legislation hurt women's opportunities. So labor changed its stance. In 1973 members of the AFL-CIO union voted to endorse the ERA.

Betty Friedan leads a group of women marching in support of the Equal Rights Amendment, 1970s.

believed state governments should have that right. They thought the ERA gave too much power to the federal government.

## THE MOMENTUM STOPS

By 1977 every state had considered the ERA. In some cases, legislatures had voted on the measure more than once. However, that year only one more state gave its approval. In January 1977 Indiana became the 35th state to ratify.

That July saw the death of Alice Paul, who had worked her whole life to pass the ERA. She was in her late eighties when the campaign for ratification began. But despite her age she lobbied politicians. She made phone calls to congressmen and legislators. And she wrote letters and editorials. In 1977, at the age of 92, she died in a nursing home in New Jersey.

## EXTENDED DEADLINE

The ERA ratification deadline was March 22, 1979. As that date loomed pro-ERA groups increased their efforts. They worked to convince legislators to ratify. NOW urged groups to hold conventions only in states that had ratified the ERA. Women marched and picketed. They wrote letters and articles. And they held rallies.

But there were still 15 states that had not approved. The Illinois legislature voted on the ERA every year. The Florida, North Carolina, and Oklahoma legislatures voted multiple times. But the amendment did not pass.

On October 20, 1978, President Jimmy Carter signed a controversial bill extending the deadline for ratification of the Equal Rights Amendment by 39 months. Despite the additional time, ERA supporters could not secure the three state legislature approvals needed to make the amendment part of the U.S. Constitution.

Meanwhile, five state legislatures voted to retract ratification. They were Nebraska (1973), Tennessee (1974), Idaho (1977), Kentucky (1978), and South Dakota (1979). The courts later ruled that states could not do this. But the ERA still needed three more states.

In July 1978 NOW sponsored a march in Washington, D.C. More than 100 thousand supporters rallied on the steps of the Capitol building. They called on Congress to extend the ERA deadline. That August the House voted to approve an extension. The following October the Senate agreed. Three more years were added. The new deadline was June 30, 1982. President Carter signed the measure into law.

But in 1980 the ERA lost the support of one of the two major political parties. In 1980 the Republican Party removed the amendment from its platform. Republican presidential candidate Ronald Reagan opposed the ERA. In the elections that fall, he defeated Jimmy Carter. And he became the first U.S. president to oppose the ERA.

# FINAL DEADLINE

On June 30, 1982, ERA supporters mourned. The ratification deadline had arrived. And the necessary 38 states had not approved the amendment. That evening NOW president Eleanor Smeal comforted ERA supporters. She told them that the fight was not over. "We are a majority. We are determined to play majority politics," she said. "We are not going to be reduced again to the ladies' auxiliary."

At a party in Washington, D.C., ERA opponents celebrated. Schlafly called their success "a great victory for women."

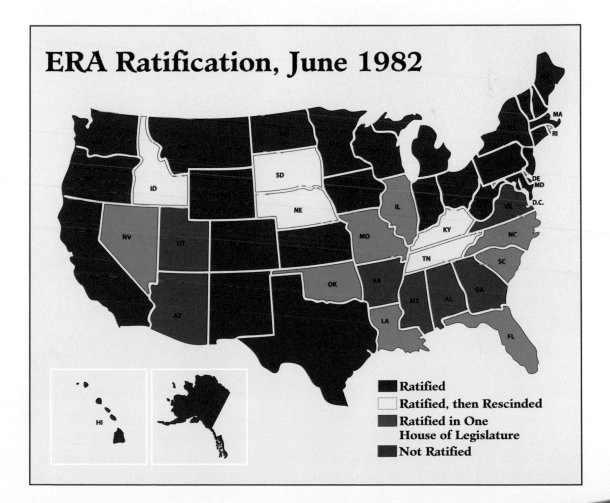

ERA Ratification, June 1982

Ratified
Ratified, then Rescinded
Ratified in One House of Legislature
Not Ratified

Although the Equal Rights Amendment has not yet been ratified, other laws passed in the 1970s and 1980s have leveled the playing field for women. Title IX of the Education Amendments of 1972 required schools that received federal funds to open all programs and activities to both male and female students. This provided greater educational opportunities to women, particularly in professions like law and medicine.

# 5

# WOMEN IN THE CONSTITUTION

Two weeks after ratification of the ERA failed, the amendment came back to life. On July 14, 1982, House representative Peter Rodino introduced the amendment in the House. Senator Paul Tsongas introduced it in the Senate. Outside on the Capitol steps, supporters rallied in the summer heat. One held a banner saying "ERA Won't Go Away." Another sign demanded "Put Women in the Constitution."

The House did not debate the measure right away. In November 1983, there was a vote. It was 278 for and 147 against. To achieve a two-thirds majority, the ERA needed 284 yes votes. The amendment failed by a 6-vote margin.

The ERA continues to be introduced before every session of Congress. But it has not been debated or voted on. It has remained in committee. If passed by the House and Senate, the amendment would have to go through the process of ratification. That is, it would require approval by 38 states.

## WHY DID IT FAIL?

Some people believe the ERA failed because its supporters were too divided. NOW and ERAmerica both worked for ratification. But they did not always work together. They held separate fundraising and political activities. And they did not agree on strategy and tactics.

The two groups were very different. NOW was confrontational. It organized protests. It held mass rallies and marches. Such tactics brought media attention. But they sometimes created negative feelings with the public. ERAmerica was less confrontational. But it was not unified. The mostly volunteer group had representatives from hundreds of organizations. So its messages were not consistent. And it was also not well organized at the grassroots level. So it did not get its message out to the community.

On the other hand, anti-ERA groups had a strong grassroots organization. They worked effectively at local and state levels. They produced publications and handouts to get their message to the public. Brochures instilled fears about the changes ERA could cause. And Phyllis Schlafly served as an effective spokesperson.

Anti-ERA groups turned the debate over the ERA into one of family values. Their message was that the amendment was bad for families. And more people came to believe that the ERA would be harmful. Public opinion changed from supporting the amendment to opposing it. And state legislators voted accordingly.

## LEGISLATIVE GAINS

Although the ERA did not become law, the debate over it fostered change. Many women's concerns came to the public's attention. During the 1970s Congress passed laws that addressed issues of sex discrimination.

# FAST FACT

During the 1960s many women were not allowed into graduate school. In 2010 the U.S. Census reported that more women than men had advanced college degrees. There were 10.6 million U.S. women with master's degrees or higher. Men numbered 10.5 million.

Before Title IX, less than 4 percent of girls played varsity high school sports. Today, that figure is more than 40 percent. At the college level, athletic scholarships for women were extremely rare prior to Title IX. Now, Division I schools award more than $1 million in scholarships to women annually.

One important law was Title IX. It is part of the Education Amendments of 1972. Title IX prohibits discrimination on the basis of gender in educational programs or activities using federal funding. It means that schools have to treat men and women equally.

Title IX opened doors for women in colleges and graduate programs. Schools could no longer refuse to admit women. And their numbers increased. In 1970 only 8.4 percent of medical school graduates were women. By the end of the decade, the number was 23 percent. In 1970 only 5.4 percent of graduates from law school were women. In 1979, 28.5 percent were women.

Title IX also affected women in sports. Coed schools had to sponsor both men's and women's teams. As a result, female athletes gained more opportunities to play for their high school or college.

In April 2010 Jacqueline A. Berrien became chairperson of the U.S. Equal Employment Opportunity Commission. The EEOC enforces federal laws that prohibit discrimination in both the federal government and in private companies.

Congress addressed discrimination in the workplace with the Equal Employment Opportunity Act. In 1972 the Act gave the EEOC enforcement power. This meant the agency had power to sue in court. The law helped stop workplace discrimination.

The Equal Credit Opportunity Act of 1974 prohibited discrimination based on sex or marital status. This meant a married woman could walk into a bank and open an account in her name. She could sign up for a credit card in her name. Or she could take out a loan. Before then, banks could require a husband's signature before extending credit. Or a department store could cancel a woman's credit card if she got divorced.

## POLITICAL GAINS

Women also became more visible in politics. Some had been pro-ERA supporters. Others had opposed the amendment. Both sides had worked within the political system. And they decided to join it.

During the 1980s many women ran for political offices. Some became mayors. Others were elected to state legislatures. And some were elected

# FAST FACT

In 1963 women were making 59 cents for every dollar a man made. In 2010 women made 77 cents for every dollar a man made.

to federal office. Participation in federal government grew. In 1973 women made up just 3.7 percent of the House of Representatives. In 1993 the number was 10.8 percent. In the Senate, the number went from zero to 6 percent. In 2011 women made up about 17 percent of both chambers.

Ideas about women were also changing. During the 1960s few people thought that a woman could be U.S. president. But in the decades that followed, several women ran for the highest office. In 1972 Shirley Chisholm was the first African-American woman to campaign. In 1988 Patricia Schroeder attempted to win the nomination. And in 2007 Hillary Rodham Clinton launched a strong campaign.

Women also appeared on the ticket as vice-president. In 1984 the Democratic Party nominated Geraldine Ferraro to run as vice president. She was the first woman to be nominated as vice president by a major political party. In 2008 Sarah Palin became the first Republican vice presidential candidate.

More than 18 million people voted for Hillary Rodham Clinton during the 2008 Democratic Party primary.

## STATE ERAS

The ERA remained alive in many states. During the 1970s 15 states included equal rights for women in their constitutions. Today, more than one-third of all U.S. states feature a version of the ERA. Some people believe such laws have had a major impact on sex discrimination lawsuits in state courts.

But pro-ERA activists say state ERAs are not enough. They claim that state courts can interpret the laws differently. As a result, women are not protected from discrimination. ERA supporters say a federal amendment is still needed.

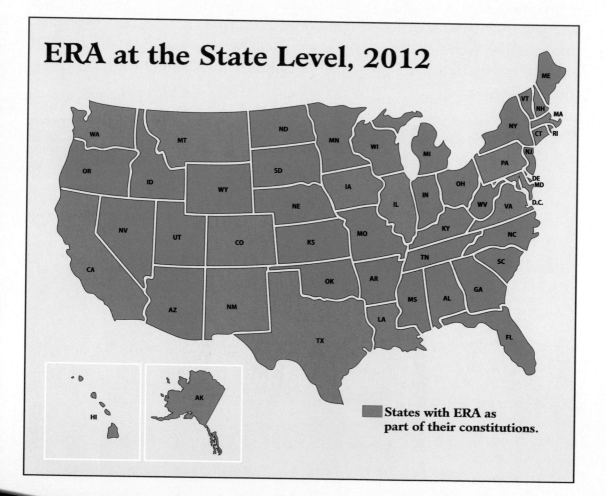

## ERA at the State Level, 2012

States with ERA as part of their constitutions.

# THREE-STATE STRATEGY

Some lawyers argue that ratifying the original ERA is possible. They say that Congress can still amend the deadline for ratification. There is a precedent. Congress amended the deadline in 1978. At that time it extended the time limit by three years. This means the legislative body has the power to change previously established deadlines.

There is another reason why legal experts think ratification is still possible. In 1789 Congress passed an amendment that prevented sitting members of Congress from voting themselves a pay raise. Any approved pay raises would not take effect until the following session. The measure was called the Madison Amendment. More than 200 years passed before the Madison Amendment was ratified. In 1992 it became the Twenty-Seventh Amendment. Ratification after so many years could mean that amendments should have no ratification deadlines. (The Constitution sets no time limit for ratification of amendments.)

This thinking, legal experts say, means the original ERA can still be ratified. All that is needed is for three more states to approve the amendment. This is known as the three-state strategy. Once three more states agree ERA supporters will go back to Congress. And they will argue to have the time limit removed.

One ERA supporter in Florida was state senator Gwen Margolis. In 2003 she tried to push a ratification bill through. "It's important to give women equal rights within the Constitution," Margolis told the *New York Times*. "I don't think women are treated equally, and to have a constitutional guarantee is very, very significant."

# FAST FACT

In 2011 New Jersey Senator Robert Menendez claimed that three-fourths of Americans believe the ERA is already part of the Constitution.

U.S. Rep. Carolyn B. Maloney of New York has reintroduced the Equal Rights Amendment in the House of Representatives during every session of Congress since 2000.

By 2007 ratification resolutions had been introduced in the legislatures of eight states. But as of 2011 no states had fully ratified. That February the Virginia Senate voted it approval. But the Virginia House refused to vote.

## RENEWED CONCERNS

In the U.S. House of Representatives, Carolyn B. Maloney has reintroduced the ERA several times. In 2003 she said, "Judges and elected officials come and go, but the Constitution is forever. We need to have the basic principles of women's equality in the Constitution."

Concerns about legal rights of women resurfaced in December 2010. That month Supreme Court justice Antonin Scalia gave an interview to a law magazine. In the publication he voiced his opinion that the Constitution does not prohibit discrimination based on gender. "Certainly the Constitution does not require discrimination on the basis of sex," he said. "The only issue is whether it prohibits it. It doesn't."

The Supreme Court is the final authority on U.S. law. In 1971 the Court had ruled in favor of women in a sex discrimination case. And it based its decision on the Fourteenth Amendment. That amendment guarantees all citizens equal rights. But the comment by Justice Scalia showed that he did not agree.

In December 2010 Senator Robert Menendez had introduced the ERA in the Senate. After Scalia's comments were published, Menendez made a public statement promoting the need for the amendment. He stated, "Justice

Scalia's recent comments have made it crystal clear that until equal protection for women is explicitly spelled out in the Constitution, the courts might not guarantee it."

Menendez was joined by Congresswoman Tammy Baldwin of Wisconsin. In March 2011 she and seven cosponsors introduced legislation in the U.S. House. The proposed bill called for removing the ERA ratification deadline. "The ERA is intended to ensure equality for women and men in all areas of society," said Baldwin. "Achieving equality and justice for all in the United States is fundamental to our democratic principles . . . and continued leadership around the world." If passed, the law would mean only three more states would be needed to ratify the ERA.

"It is a disgrace that American women are still not constitutionally guaranteed equal rights under the law," said Senator Robert Menendez in June 2011. "Women have made tremendous advancements in our society, but we must continue to advance women's rights by bringing our laws in line with 21st century values."

## ATTITUDES TODAY

U.S. society has changed. Many issues originally brought forth by anti-ERA activists are widely accepted by the public today. Women in the 21st century willingly serve in the military. Same-sex civil unions are legal in many states. There are fewer traditional two-parent families, too. The U.S. Census Bureau reported in 1980 that 77 percent of children under the age of 17 lived in a traditional two-parent family. By 2008 that number had fallen to 67 percent.

Still, some people today believe an ERA is not needed. They think women's rights are protected already. But others argue that the laws in place to protect women from sex discrimination are not working. They continue to call for women to be acknowledged as equals in the U.S. Constitution. And they insist that only an Equal Rights Amendment would do that.

# CHAPTER NOTES

p. 10: "It is incredible to . . ." Alice Paul, quoted in "Women's Party to Call a Convention," *New York Times*, September 11, 1920.

p. 11: "Men and women shall have . . ." Alice Paul, quoted in Susan Ware, ed. *Notable American Women: A Biographical Dictionary* (Cambridge, Mass.: Belknap Press of Harvard University Press, 2004), 502.

p. 12: "We shall not be safe . . ." Alice Paul, quoted in Sibyl A. Schwarzenbach and Patricia Smith, eds. *Women and the United States Constitution* (New York: Columbia University Press, 2003), 350.

p. 12: "in order to bring . . ." Alice Paul, quoted in Amelia R. Fry, "Suffragists Oral History Project: Conversations with Alice Paul: Woman Suffrage and the Equal Rights Amendment," University of California, November 1972 and May 1973. http://texts.cdlib.org/view?docId=kt6f59n89c&doc.view=frames&chunk.id=d0e20361&toc.id=d0e27384&brand=calisphere&query=alice%20paul

p. 19: "[P]rotective legislation that is . . ." National Woman's Party, quoted in Ruth Bader Ginsburg, "The Need for the Equal Rights Amendment," *ABA Journal*, September 1973, 1018.

p. 21: "Equality of rights under . . ." Ginsburg, "The Need for the Equal Rights Amendment," 1013.

p. 21: "So it was substituted . . ." Paul, quoted in Fry, "Suffragists Oral History Project: Conversations with Alice Paul: Woman Suffrage and the Equal Rights Amendment."

p. 21: "We favor submission by Congress . . ." Republican Party Platform of 1940 (June 24, 1940). http://www.presidency.ucsb.edu/ws/index.php?pid=29640#axzz1bvQFcziU

p. 22: "specific bills for . . ." Schwarzenbach and Patricia Smith, eds. *Women and the United States Constitution*, 350.

p. 24: "very, *very* friendly to the cause of women," Paul, quoted in Fry, "Suffragists Oral History Project: Conversations with Alice Paul: Woman Suffrage and the Equal Rights Amendment.

p. 25: "The husband is head . . ." Ginsburg, "The Need for the Equal Rights Amendment," 1014.

p. 27: "The problem that has no name," Betty Friedan, *The Feminine Mystique*

(New York: W. W. Norton and Co., 1963), 63.

p. 28: "the present troublesome . . ." Esther Peterson, quoted in Jo Freeman, *We Will Be Heard: Women's Struggles For Political Power in the United States* (Lanham, Md.: Rowman & Littlefield, 2008), 175.

p. 29: "nor shall any state . . ." Amendment XIV, "The Charters of Freedom: Constitution of the United States, Amendments 11–27." http://www.archives.gov/exhibits/charters/constitution_amendments_11-27.html

p. 30: "another minority group, the women." Howard Smith, quoted in Freeman, *We Will Be Heard*, 171.

p. 30: "I presume that if . . ." Martha Griffiths, quoted in Nancy MacLean, *Freedom Is Not Enough: The Opening of the American Workplace* (Harvard University Press, 2008), 121.

p. 30: "Give us a chance . . ." Martha Griffiths, quoted in Leslie W. Gladstone, "The Long Road to Equality: What Women Won from the ERA Ratification Effort," Library of Congress American Memory: American Women, 2001. http://memory.loc.gov/ammem/awhhtml/aw03e/aw03c.html

p. 32: "The adoption of a blunderbuss . . ." Emanuel Celler, quoted in Gladstone, "Notes: The Long Road to Equality" http://memory.loc.gov/ammem/awhhtml/aw03e/notes.html

p. 33: "Sec. 1. Equality of rights . . ." Ginsburg, "The Need for the Equal Rights Amendment," 1013.

Women march through Washington, D.C., demanding equality, August 26, 1970. The National Organization for Women (NOW) planned this march.

p. 34: "In this Land of . . ." Gerald Ford, August 26, 1975 proclamation quoted in "The Equal Rights Amendment," 4ERA. http://www.4era.org

p. 39: "anti-family, anti-children, . . ." Phyllis Schlafly, quoted in Donald T. Critchlow and Cynthia L. Stachecki, "The Equal Rights Amendment Reconsidered: Politics, Policy, and Social Mobilization in a Democracy," *Journal of Policy History* 20 (2008): 166.

p. 43: "We are a majority . . ." Eleanor Smeal, quoted in Hays Gorey, Jane O'Reilly, and Anastasia Toufexis, "What Killed Equal Rights?" *Time*, July 12, 1982.

p. 43: "a great victory for . . ." Phyllis Schlafly, quoted in Elisabeth Bumiller, "Schlafly's Gala Goodbye to ERA," *Washington Post*, July 1, 1982, C-1.

p. 51: "It's important to give . . ." Gwen Margolis, quoted in Dana Canedy, "Advocates of Equal Rights Amendment Resume Their Fight," *New York Times*, May 4, 2003.

p. 52: "Judges and elected . . . " Carolyn B. Maloney, quoted in Canedy, "Advocates of Equal Rights Amendment Resume Their Fight."

p. 52: "Certainly the Constitution . . ." Antonin Scalia, quoted in Paul Courson, "Scalia Comments Show Need for New Rights Amendment, Backers Say," CNN, January 6, 2011. http://articles.cnn.com/2011-01-06/politics/era.scalia_1_constitution-14th-amendment-equal-rights-amendment?_s=PM:POLITICS

p. 52: "Justice Scalia's recent . . ." Robert Menendez, quoted in "As Constitution Is Read Aloud, Menendez, Maloney, Nadler, Moore Cite Need for Equal Rights Amendment," press release, January 6, 2011. http://menendez.senate.gov/newsroom/press/release/?id=5258013d-3c02-454f-b784-0b62e57b68fc

p. 53: "The ERA is intended . . ." Tammy Baldwin, quoted in "Baldwin Seeks to Speed Ratification of Equal Rights Amendment (ERA)," press release, March 8, 2011. http://tammybaldwin.house.gov/legislativeissues/women/2011/03/baldwin-seeks-to-speed-ratification-of-equal-rights-amendment-era.shtml

p. 53: "It is a disgrace . . ." Robert Menendez, "Rep. Maloney, Sen. Menendez reintroduce the Equal Rights Amendment," (June 22, 2011). http://menendez.senate.gov/newsroom/press/release/?id=65b84343-9eed-4433-ae32-03a5e98618b4

# CHRONOLOGY

**1848:** The first women's rights convention meets in Seneca Falls, New York; its members call for political and legal equality.

**1916:** The National Woman's Party is founded.

**1919:** The National American Suffrage Association becomes the League of Women Voters.

**1920:** The 19th Amendment, which gives women the vote, is ratified; the National Woman's Party turns to working for legal equality for women.

**1923:** Alice Paul cowrites the Equal Rights Amendment; it is introduced into Congress.

**1938:** The Fair Labor Standards Act is passed.

**1940:** The Republican Party endorses the ERA as part of its platform.

**1941:** The United States enters World War II; women take jobs traditionally held by men.

**1943:** The original Equal Rights Amendment is rewritten.

**1944:** The Democratic Party includes the ERA in its platform.

**1945:** World War II ends; many women workers lose their jobs to returning soldiers.

**1946:** The ERA is debated on the Senate floor; it fails to pass.

**1950:** After the Hayden rider is added, the ERA passes the Senate, but it is not brought to a vote in the House.

**1961:** President John F. Kennedy establishes the President's Commission on the Status of Women (PCSW).

**1963:** Betty Friedan publishes *The Feminine Mystique*; the PCSW report *American Women* is published.

**1964:** Title VII of the Civil Rights Act prohibits employment discrimination based on sex.

**1966:** The National Organization for Women is founded.

**1972:** Title IX of the Education Amendment of the Civil Rights Act prohibits discrimination on the basis of sex; Phyllis Schlafly founds the Eagle Forum; the ERA passes both houses of Congress.

**1976:** The ratification campaign organization ERAmerica is founded in Washington, D.C.

**1977:** By January, 35 states have ratified the ERA; in October, Congress approves a measure to extend the seven-year deadline by three more years; in November, the first National Women's Conference takes place in Houston, Texas.

**1982:** The June 30 deadline for ratification of the ERA expires; on July 14, the amendment is reintroduced in Congress.

**1983 to present:** The Equal Rights Amendment is introduced in each subsequent session of Congress.

# GLOSSARY

**amendment**—a legal change to the U.S. Constitution.

**civil rights**—the rights of a citizen to political and social freedom and equality.

**coalition**—a union formed among organizations.

**discrimination**—the unjust or prejudicial treatment of people based on sex, race, religion, age, or another category.

**federal**—relating to the central government of the United States.

**feminism**—the advocacy of achieving social, political, and economic equality between the sexes.

**grassroots**—the basic level of membership of a group or organization.

**lobbyist**—a person who works to influence politicians or public officials on a particular issue.

**preamble**—introduction.

**ratification**—the act of giving formal consent to a measure; the act of making it officially valid.

**suffrage**—the right to vote.

# FURTHER READING

## FOR YOUNGER READERS

Attebury, Nancy Garhan. *Gloria Steinem: Champion of Women's Rights*. Minneapolis, Minn.: Compass Point Books, 2006.

Baker, Jean H. *Sisters: The Lives of America's Suffragists*. New York: Hill and Wang, 2005.

LaDuke, Aaron J., ed. *Living through the Sexual Revolution*. Detroit : Greenhaven Press, Thomson Gale, 2006.

Schomp, Virginia. *The Women's Movement*. New York: Marshall Cavendish Benchmark, 2007.

Wright, Susan. *The Civil Rights Act of 1964: Landmark Antidiscrimination Legislation*. New York: Rosen Pub. Group, 2006.

## FOR OLDER READERS

Critchlow, Donald T. *Phyllis Schlafly and Grassroots Conservatism: A Woman's Crusade*. Princeton, N.J.: Princeton University Press, 2005.

Stansell, Christine. *The Feminist Promise: 1792 to the Present*. New York: Modern Library, 2010.

Strebeigh, Fred. *Equal: Women Reshape American Law*. New York: W. W. Norton, 2009.

Walton, Mary. *A Woman's Crusade: Alice Paul and the Battle for the Ballot*. New York: Palgrave Macmillan, 2010.

# INTERNET RESOURCES

## http://www.equalrightsamendment.org

This website features background information on the ERA. It also includes updated information on the ERA's current status in the U.S. Congress and in unratified states.

## http://www.sewallbelmont.org

The Sewall-Belmont House was the home of the National Woman's Party and is now a museum. Its website links to information documenting the effort to win the vote. It also features information on Alice Paul and the campaign to win legal equality for women.

## http://www.eagleforum.org/era/index.html

Phyllis Schlafly's Eagle Forum website features links to information on its reasons for opposing passage of the ERA.

## http://www.alicepaul.org

This official website of the Alice Paul Institute features links to information on Paul and her childhood home, known as Paulsdale.

## http://memory.loc.gov/ammem/awhhtml/aw03e/aw03e.html

This site features a Library of Congress essay on American women. Text and photos make up "The Long Road to Equality: What Women Won from the ERA Ratification Effort."

# INDEX

Numbers in **bold italics** refer to captions.

# CONTRIBUTORS

**LeeAnne Gelletly** is the author of several books for young adults, including biographies of Harriet Beecher Stowe, Mae Jemison, Roald Dahl, Ida Tarbell, and John Marshall.

Senior Consulting Editor **A. Page Harrington** is executive director of the Sewall-Belmont House and Museum, on Capitol Hill in Washington, D.C. The Sewall-Belmont House celebrates women's progress toward equality—and explores the evolving role of women and their contributions to society—through educational programs, tours, exhibits, research, and publications.

The historic National Woman's Party (NWP), a leader in the campaign for equal rights and women's suffrage, owns, maintains, and interprets the Sewall-Belmont House and Museum. One of the premier women's history sites in the country, this National Historic Landmark houses an extensive collection of suffrage banners, archives, and artifacts documenting the continuing effort by women and men of all races, religions, and backgrounds to win voting rights and equality for women under the law.

The Sewall-Belmont House and Museum and the National Woman's Party are committed to preserving the legacy of Alice Paul, founder of the NWP and author of the Equal Rights Amendment, and telling the untold stories for the benefit of scholars, current and future generations of Americans, and all the world's citizens.